MY
MANY MEs
AND
MORE
DISORDERS

and how to unlock the true YOU

Natasha Kons

First Printed: 2017

ISBN 978-0-6481543-0-3

Published in Australia by Natasha Kons in 2017
PO Box 677, East Bentleigh VIC 3167, Australia

www.natashakons.com
nkonsmmm@gmail.com

Cover design and image by Natasha Kons

Ordering Information:
Special discounts are available on quantity purchases by corporations, associations, educators, and others. For details, contact the publisher at the above listed address.

For Max... fly high ∞

Knowing her wonderful family, I have always felt that Natasha has been well-equipped to venture forth in life with creativity, fortitude and just the right amount of humility. She is incredibly loved. She is also intuitive and kind and her personal conviction is her solidity.

I have had the immense pleasure of her friendship over fourteen years and have recently been inaugurated as her aunty, a role I gladly accept with great pride and affection.

Yet this relationship has also made it very hard to watch her going through the challenges she has endured - I have seen her struggle with physical and emotional pain - and have felt powerless to help and devastated to see her suffering. She has wrestled with seizures, interactions with entities and the spirit world, and health care workers who misunderstood and misdiagnosed.

However through it all, Natasha has emerged unbroken. She has taken her experiences and unleashed a fierce determination to understand herself. Natasha has chosen to do what many of us, even as adults, can't or won't do - fight against a tide of conformity and apathy. She has constantly challenged commonly held theories and beliefs, particularly with regard to medical 'diagnoses', until she has finally come to the path which shines bright for her.

That is no small thing for someone so young. She is an inspiration - she shows us the importance of being brave enough to defy the status quo and implicitly trust your instincts about what is right for you - leading to clarity, self-love...and freedom.

Petrina Ley

Contents

Acknowledgements

My deepest gratitude and love goes to
my mum, number one supporter
and inspiration.

Thank you to my sisters;
Maddie, for being my rock when things go shaky
and Sophia for her quirkiness,
my dad for always seeing the fun and
lightness in everything.

Libby Gordon, my Fairy Godmother and
Grant Lambert for bringing clarity and
healing into my life and for his contribution
to my blurb.
Petrina Ley for being a nurturing and
caring aunty who stepped in as a mother
figure in crucial times.
Lachie Campbell and Jasmine Bennett
for everlasting and true friendship.
Colin Steele for his inspiration and belief in me.

*Thanks to Sara and Solomon,
the characters of the Sara* series
by Esther and Jerry Hicks.*

I wouldn't be here without YOU.

A little note from me

Countless books have been written on laws
of attraction and so called self-help books, so
my contribution is only one
of my own experience.
All I want to achieve with my point of
view on several subjects is that YOU
understand that the only person or thing in
charge is
YOU.

And no matter how much you read or listen
to, know that all knowledge is just borrowed
knowledge.
Go out and experience everything yourself.
Do your own research on anything
concerning YOU.
Don't wait for a saviour or listen to a guru,
another marketing campaign that tries to
sell you the latest wonder pill, cream,
philosophy, etc. because
You are an individual, totally responsible for
your own destiny,
your very own
TRUTH.

Let's not judge, nor label.
*Let it just **Be**.*

My Story

I began conversing with spirits when I started Kindergarten. I remember it very clearly. My imaginary friends were many. I excitedly told my parents about my experiences in great detail. They politely listened; enjoying my story-telling abilities but their response was quite disheartening, as they didn't join in with my excitement. I felt misunderstood so I kept my adventures to myself.

Often sitting with a wise old man, I expressed my anguish about kindergarten and the daily dramas I encountered. He always listened patiently and I asked him endless questions about everything and anything. He never replied with the answer I so wanted to hear. He only ever responded with saying: "You shall know soon enough" and "what you feel in your heart to be right – is so". I thought to myself, "why aren't you giving me more constructive feedback – seriously!?

However, our talks made me feel secure and safe. Although he was not physically in existence, I always knew it was for the best, him not being in human form. Who else has a wise old man on call whenever you please? No bookings, no problem.

Even back then I felt people on a different level; energetically and intuitively. Most people's sad and negative thoughts and experiences would overwhelm me. I could see into their past, present and future, becoming one with their soul, gaining insight into their personal nature and experiences. People would always say: "You don't know what I went through…" – oh mate...but I did. I somehow, not knowing how, gained the ability to receive quick information transfers of feelings and images, a like to telepathy.

At the time I didn't really give it much thought; I just took it as truth. It was just what it was and made me feel real good, therefore didn't have time to discard anything about it as being unreal.

In primary school I was bullied and I started doubting their existence, as they should have come to my rescue.

Whoever I told about my funny entourage would smile at me with a very sorry look on their face for not knowing better that such things did not exist and everyone told me that I was quite the story teller.

Since being diagnosed with dyslexia, my mum was rather prejudice about the whole thing. Something didn't really add up right…

Over time, I forgot about it, as people had made me believe that I was weaving lies.

I somehow got through primary school and landed face down in High School. Year 7 to 9 was really tough on me. You might relate to this or not, but school, in general, was not one of my places of interest. I very much loathed it.

All those years of being tormented, I accepted all the narcissistic garbage (a bit harsh I know...but that's the truth), the other girls and boys had said to me, destroying my very being with each and every spiteful word. The power of the spoken word can do much damage, literally making me, and anyone really, feel physically effected. Remarks like me being too 'dumb' to too 'fat', that I was a 'waste of space' and that 'no one could ever love me'...on and on those comments would infect my little brain and would make me feel so hopeless – particularly when I was forced by one of the girls into the bins in the playground.

Trying to get away from it all, I thought it might be a good idea to move schools, which in hindsight, wasn't any help either. The problems wouldn't go away but stay the same or even got worse.

I realised then that I was purely trying to avoid school altogether, never wanting to face any dramas again. All I wanted was to be happy and since I never felt like I belonged, all I wanted was to escape – school, life – anything to get away from it all.

My hard-hitting year, emotionally, was at thirteen. I had heavy, negative thoughts and there was so much going on in my head that the only way to handle that influx of information and pondering, was to write about it (lol … I'm dyslexic).

I wrote and wrote and scribbled on every piece of paper I could find. Reading back on it now, I always end up crying, as the feeling of the isolation I felt at that time was so heavy and horrible; making it hard for me to breathe. I used writing as a means of releasing this bundle of sadness and solitude I felt, hoping the pages would listen and somehow save me and absorb the pain.

Even in the comfort of my home and knowing that I was very much loved, I was enveloped by darkness. I felt tired and worthless. Most days I was thinking, what would happen if I was gone?

There was not a single day I didn't have thoughts about ending it all. I couldn't talk to anyone because I felt ashamed and totally out of place.

I withdrew more and more, was very quiet and spent much too much time in my room. I tried talking to my mum but her response was discouraging so I kept to myself. She didn't understand how tormented I felt and believed that I should stay in the positive and appreciate all that is, and that people had it much harder than me.

I pulled back and promised myself I would never say another word, just to keep the peace and not to worry my family. Also, I did not want to add any more drama to our lives, as my parents were having a tough time themselves. We had lost our house since business was tough and sometimes the tension in the house was a little heavy and too much for all of us.

My mum started worrying about my state of being and sought help with a professional. I was diagnosed with depression, anxiety and agoraphobia. I had an extreme fear of death whenever I went outside of my comfort zone at home. My bedroom provided me with security. The isolation and protection in those four walls made it easier - no one could get to me there.

My peers were totally oblivious and would have never thought what I was going through. I was hiding my emotions and acted as if nothing was wrong. I felt confused, couldn't see the point in anything - I was very much lost. Nevertheless, I pushed on somehow and kept my head above water.

Then one day when I was in Year 9, my mum came home with an audio book called 'Sara' by Esther and Jerry Hicks.

The blurb reads:
"This book offers you, the reader, a thoughtful and inspired formula for generating appreciation, happiness, and good feelings - deftly blended into the uplifting story of a plucky, inquisitive girl named Sara; and her teacher, an ethereal owl named Solomon. There's something in Sara for any child, adult, or teen pursuing joy and meaning...and searching for

answers about life, death, and the desires of the heart. It's filled with techniques and processes for making one's dreams come true...especially yours! Sara and Solomon will delight and enchant you!"

Listening to this story, again and again, changed my life completely and turned everything around for me and I began to view the world in a very different light.

It was all about the power of appreciation and gratitude, the Law of attraction and so much more. I was so stimulated and grateful.

I started to put everything the story conveyed into practice. The results created such a shift for me as life began to blossom and illustrate the unfoldment of beauty in life. I felt a part of the voyages life had to offer. I rapidly excelled in anything I put my mind and heart to. I began to understand that I was the creator of my life and the situations I found myself in.

Every morning I said to myself that I was going to have the best day ever. While walking to school I started appreciating every little thing I could think of. From the bins on the side of the road providing a place to throw all our rubbish in, to the friendly dog behind the fence wagging his tail giving a warm greeting to passers-by.

My perspective of my surroundings changed

immensely and I was having the best time ever.
At nights when I was supposed to be doing my
homework I would stay up and watch inspirational
videos on YouTube about how the Laws of Attraction
worked. Every time I listened to talks and watched
more of anything related to this subject, a rush of
excitement ran through my body and I felt so happy
and elated; something familiar stirred in me.

My life took on a different dimension and I had a lot
of fun. It seemed that luck was on my side and life was
flowing easily. I felt good, really good and happy.

I went from Enduring to Enjoyment.

Bit by bit, over the next two years, I tried harder
at school and somewhat achieved better results, even
though inconsistently. I was mainly doing things for
fun and seriously enjoyed myself being a teenager. My
core focus was not school but my own well-being, I
made sure that whatever was going on, I was looking
after myself.

Schools don't really teach you about self-care and
self-love and the importance of it all. School-work
is always Number One. As long as you do well and
achieve the necessary results and conform to the rules
and regulations, that's all it takes. Sadly, this leaves
many of us grappling behind emotionally.

With so many young people coming from broken

homes and facing many challenges from a very early age, they are lost and are lacking stability and appropriate role-modelling. They are usually confronted with too many issues that shouldn't really be theirs to carry and deal with. And as society becomes more and more complex, de-fragmented and unstable, life is becoming more unsettled for us young ones.

There were many instances where I started questioning the motives of some of my teachers and other staff. Too often I observed a power play that was being carried out and left me wondering what they tried to achieve with almost 'bullying' students into conformity. At home we learned all about mutual respect and my mum is a big advocate of it. During Karate lessons we were taught about seniority, that you have to respect your elders. At the same time, this respect needs to be earned and not be expected. It's all about living by example. But there weren't many teachers I was looking up to or felt inspired by. Too many seemed to be dragging their feet and just 'doing a job', not having their heart and soul in it.

Do teachers' beliefs influence how
students perform?
Studies have confirmed that obvious question!

When teachers were led to believe that
their students were intellectually gifted,
the students' performance improved.
Because the teachers' behaviour
towards *them* changed.

So how do we get teachers to have the
right beliefs, which will then create the
right behaviours?

-

Tom Asacker,
The Business of Belief

I was told what subjects I could or could not chose and was given a list of career paths that I could pursue with the marks I had achieved in the few subjects that I was able to undertake. Since I went to a public school, subjects and opportunities were limited and therefore put me and my fellow students already into yet another category.

I started realising that school is just another broken system. I felt limited in my choices and belittled as I was told what career path was open to me, according to my marks only. School was dislocating me from my true talents and my passion for subjects that weren't taught at my school (or any school for that matter).

At home, in my own time, I was listening a lot to TED talks which I found on the internet (TED is a non-profit devoted to spreading ideas, usually in the form of short, powerful talks) and other amazing innovative thinkers. I also read up about crystals and their powers to heal as all this was starting to become important to me. I even started to understand physics through my interest in all things mystical and wondrous. Turns out that Quantum physics explains a lot that can't really be explained and does not make sense when not understood. Anything really that the so called 'normal people' didn't really talk about nor take into consideration. To me, this opened up a whole new world and I felt very much at ease.

I was puzzled about the hypocrisy of it all.

It became harder and harder for me to conform to the education system. I also had trouble relating to my peers and a growing feeling of not belonging again started to rise up.

At one point I just couldn't justify going to school any longer. I desperately began to search for avenues to get out of school at all cost. At home I started talking about running my own café one day or to learn a trade because I wanted to build my very own house. I racked my brain to find suitable excuses for leaving school since my dad wanted me to finish school and do the right thing for my future. His motto was: "When you finish VCE you can do anything you like!"

But I didn't want to finish school as I saw no point in it. Besides I always knew that I wasn't going to finish school with VCE. I was convinced that I needed to do it my way.

I found myself torn though, wanting to please my dad so badly as I knew that he only wanted the best for me. I totally understood his point of view – he only did what he knew best and what he had come to believe to be the right way. But he had no idea about the harm he inflicted on me with his stern conviction of forcing me into finishing school with VCE. My mum was pretty cool about it and very supportive which gave me some sort of reassurance to pursue my stubbornness. It was a testing time as I had to keep manoeuvring through every day, trying to avoid the

Human communities
depend on
a diversity of talent
not a singular conception of ability

-

Sir Ken Robinson;
'Bring on the learning revolution'

subject but somehow having to come to the end result, namely getting out of school.

At the end of Year 10 I was desperate and needed to get out. Always on the lookout, I surfed the internet about different trades and off I went with my friend to check out bricklaying at TAFE. Walking through the facilities, I was very impressed and I could easily see myself doing hands-on work. I could be one step closer to fulfilling my dream of building my own house and mainly to get out of school-really!

I told my mum that Bricklaying was what I wanted to do and she was happy about my enthusiasm for it. Then I tried to convince my dad, which was a different story all together again. My dad upholds his Greek traditions very much and can be very intimidating as the dominant and only male figure in our family. It seemed that he felt personally insulted and got very angry and warned me how hard and difficult it would be for me as a girl to survive out on a work-site in a male-dominated environment. He was very protective of me which I understood, but his negativity and unfounded threats were making me feel very hurt. I knew I could stand up for myself if needed.

As much as I tried everything to convince him that I needed to do a trade, as much did he try to convince me not to, it all unfolded into a real drama – a kind of 'Never Ending story'. I wouldn't give up and neither would he. My mum wanted me to be happy and had endless discussions with my dad, trying to convince him to let me do an apprenticeship in whatever trade I chose.

Mum was my rock, she stood by me and my endeavours. Eventually, after many weeks and months of arguing back and forth, we somehow got through to him and he agreed to come to an open day at TAFE in Chadstone.

I was the only girl present that day and when they repeated that bricklaying was challenging everyone seemed to glance over at me. The facilitator wanted to make sure that we (and it felt like he was directly referring to me) understood that it was real hard work, tough on the body and that not many people would keep at it for

exactly those reasons. The more he spoke about it, the more I wanted to do it and at the end of the presentation he had me, and even my dad was convinced that bricklaying might be the way to go for me, especially since job opportunities were very promising and that girls were often preferred choices by some employers, due to their diligence.

I was wrapped that dad was positive and we signed up for the course on the spot.

At the end of January we still hadn't heard from TAFE and we found out that the course wouldn't come together. After some investigation I was able to do a week trial to gain some basic skills and where future employers could watch us for possible apprenticeships. I thoroughly enjoyed the physical work and excelled in building the perfect wall on my first go. Little did they know, I had sat up all night absorbing the skills of bricklaying through an informative YouTube tutorial.

Whilst visiting my grandparents that night, my chest started to hurt me, but I didn't worry too much about it as I blamed it on the extra physical activity and the breathing in of the lime and mortar mix. Coming home later that evening the pain became unbearable and my mum and my sister, Madeleine took me to the local hospital.

Whilst waiting in the waiting room my vision became cloudy and an appeared. I told my mum that I felt like I was about to faint and she organised a bed with one of the nurses so that I could lay down. Laying flat on the bed an uncontrollable jolt ran through my body, and then another. Each resulted in a more powerful jolt. I remember that it became hard for me to speak and move my arms and legs willingly. It took strength to answer the questions of my worried parents.

Suddenly, I felt like I was being detached from my core body and it was just me. My soul, floating over every being in the room. The heightened concern and sadness filled the room yet I didn't really feel that emotion within me. I was just observing, feeling complete peace. This peace I felt cannot be described through words.

All of a sudden I was being told by a male voice that I have so much to do and that it's not my time to go just yet. At that point I didn't really think too much of it and I returned back into my physical body. After half an hour I began to calm down and was told that I had experienced my first seizure.

The doctors had done all the necessary tests but couldn't find anything wrong with me. They blamed it on my nerves as this was my first day at work and that maybe I had over done it. Being released a few hours later, we went home.

I was adamant to go back to work the next day. I was able to successfully finish my trial week and I got offered a 3 year apprenticeship. They presented me with a pink bucket and a rose and welcomed me, looking forward to having me on the team.

Even though I was excited about the prospects of my apprenticeship, a feeling of doubt washed over me and I spoke to my dad about it. I told him that I only wanted to learn the skills but that I never saw myself doing this for the rest of my life. He got angry and asked me what the point was since I could have just done a labourer's job or a short course – I shouldn't be wasting my time. All through the evening we discussed different options and eventually, since I couldn't really explain myself, he made the decision for me to go back to school.

My mum was totally devastated since she had invested all this time and effort to convince my dad to let me do what I wanted which made me feel even worse. I was so disheartened and cried all night. I felt completely lost and torn. I was a mess.

The next day I had to go back to school and re-enrol. I had limited subjects available due to me leaving high school, but didn't really care anyway. However, I was able to do a VET program, meaning that I could complete a bricklaying class once a week at TAFE which eased the pain a little bit.

I did not want to be back at school and felt really depressed. I was in my English class the first day back and I distinctly remember looking out the window, and thinking to myself "is it really worth it anymore?"

One of my teachers was very worried for me. I dragged my feet and had no motivation for anything.

That same night I was lying in my bed, saddened by it all. When all of a sudden I felt a hand on my head and a voice saying "I'm here for you, it's all going to be OK"; a familiar presence I seemed to know very well. The feeling of love ran through me and I was able to fall asleep with ease.

The coming days were tough on me, but I managed to carry on always remembering the voice's encouragement. Deep in my heart I knew, everything was going to be alright.

At the same time, my mum started taking me to see Libby. My mum had seen Libby for a few months prior as she was able to help her with some of her long-term health issues.

(Libby has been in the alternative health field for well over 25 years and has covered many aspects from physical therapy, alchemy, being a teacher, counsellor, and mentor and involved in energetic therapies. After completing a Degree in Aromatherapy, she moved immediately into the Bowen Therapy field and became a practitioner/teacher in Australia. She then welcomed the skill of learning NST (an advanced learning of Bowen) and subsequently taught this technique in Australia and the US. She was a primary instigator in the Bowen therapy becoming accredited in the health fields and setting up the Australian Federation. She has extensively used alchemy (including Flower Essences) and still conducts personal counselling sessions with her ability to read the body energetically.)

I connected with her immediately and felt comfortable exploring further with her as to what was going on with me. She introduced me to EFT, also called tapping, which is a form of psychological acupressure, based on the same energy meridians used in traditional acupuncture to treat physical and emotional ailments for over five thousand years, but without the invasiveness of needles.

Months went by, and I was trying to be a normal teenager, discussing boys and mundane everyday events with my friends. I went out a lot and spent most of my time with my best friend. Every other weekend I stayed for sleep overs and much preferred spending time with her and her family than being at home. Even though we were close and we had a great time together, I could never be completely honest with her about my feelings and all that was going on inside of me.

One morning, coming home from one of my many sleep overs I started feeling very uneasy and had trouble talking, I shut down. I laid down on the floor in the living room and that's when I started convulsing again. My mum found me and we raced to our local doctor. He examined me and suggested we go straight to Monash hospital.

I was convulsing all the way to the hospital and continued for a while longer there. They hooked me up to the machines and measured for anything out of the ordinary, but again, they couldn't make any sense of it since nothing unusual showed up. Eventually, my seizures stopped and I was returning to normal, sedate state; I felt so exhausted and still couldn't speak properly, my whole body was hurting and I felt like having just completed a marathon.

The doctors were puzzled and wanted to keep me for observation and to run further tests. They asked my mum to leave so they could have a chat with me. When we were alone, the doctor suggested that I was depressed and asked if I had anxieties as this was normal for girls my age. My symptoms also indicated that I had an eating disorder. Being told all these terrible things, made me feel like shit…that would make anyone feel depressed! So did that make me a person considered to be 'Clinically depressed?' I was very upset carrying this label. He also pointed the finger at my parents and wanted to know whether they had any issues and arguments that were affecting me. I was honest and told him that yes, there were occasional altercations. He kept on making it an issue though which was utter bullshit and I had to remind him, that they were only human and people do actually have arguments. I never considered this to be abnormal or affecting me to the point that my body had to go into convulsions.

After this, they brought my mum back in and were suggesting that I had depression, anxiety and an eating disorder and that they needed to keep me overnight.

They allocated a spot for me in a 4 bed room in the Children's ward. I was feeling my old self again and was laughing with my mum about the doctors being all so serious. We were even having a giggle about the 'awesome' hospital food – especially since I was supposed to be having an eating disorder – the food was anything but nutritious. It had been a long day and I asked my mum to go home since my best friend was coming to visit me and keep me company. That night, I had a good sleep as I was so exhausted.

Before my mum came back in the morning, I experienced another seizure that only last for 45 minutes. I was visited by many specialists wanting to know how I was going and dealing with life. I was allocated an art therapist, a music therapist and a psychologist.

Later on while my mum was sitting by my bedside, doing some work on the computer, I started fitting uncontrollably again. I felt a male presence standing directly at the head of my bed holding each side of my temples. There was also a lady standing at the foot of my bed looking down at me with sympathy in her eyes. Just to clarify…not humans. I whispered to my mum that there were people with us. She looked around and told me that no one was there. Her face changed and she told me sternly, 'Tell them to go away NOW.'

The man that had been standing behind me quickly vanished, yet the lady still stood firm. The lady I saw told me that my mum needed to stand next to her at the end of my bed. I passed this on to my mum and she followed suit. The moment my mum stood by her side, a demonic form, something like black energy, appeared to be escaping the ladies' body. This black energy seemed to struggle and resist to exit. Once the dark form left the lady's body, the whole room's atmosphere and vibrations elevated, and the lady began crying. She told me to thank my mother and nodded to me slowly fading away. Straight after this unfolding, I felt multiple hands pulling the left side of my body. I heard another voice saying: "Come with us, we need you. We can help you become who you really are."

My body was still in shock from the unfamiliar movement and strains that were occurring through my body.

I told my mum that they wanted me to go with them. Through her tears she began to say "We need you here, I love you." Those words stung deep, because there was a part of me that wanted to go with them so badly, yet another part that wanted to stay, because of the love I felt from my mum and my family.

Love is so extremely powerful and its healing abilities are incredible. Love feeds the soul and has so many positive aspects that are the answer to many people's problems.

I didn't realise the impact this experience had on my mum when she told me later, that she was scared of losing me that day. It might sound strange but I knew that I needed experience this. I was never scared, it was just what it was and I felt fine afterwards.

As per usual, all examinations turned out to be normal and there seemed nothing wrong with me from a medical point of view. The only explanation left, was that I was a little crazy and had major mental issues. The term used for my type of seizures was *Psychogenic (Non-Epileptic) Seizures*, describing it as a seizure that looks like epileptic seizures, but are not caused by abnormal electrical discharge. They are stress-related or "emotional". Also known as pseudo-seizures. So glad they found another label for my 'condition'...or did they?

That night, I had sent mum home to get a bit of sleep, I lay awake for a while and I felt that something had shifted for me. I felt strangely calm and happy and very much at peace. During the day, a girl of around 7 years had joined me in the hospital room as well as a fairly new baby that was crying constantly.

It was fairly dark in the room and I suddenly saw knots located in particular areas of the young girl and baby's bodies, acting as blockages of energy. Suddenly, a golden triangle appeared connecting the 3 of us, rising up forming the shape of a pyramid.

The following morning both of them were cleared to go home.

That same day we left the hospital since medically everything was sound and there wasn't really anything they could do for me. Before I could leave, mum and I had to have a last talk with the psychologist with her entourage of 'experts' in all things not considered 'normal'.

My mum and I were led into a small room and we were given several options of how to deal with me in the future and a few names of people to work with me from here onwards. Everyone's facial expression was very dim and I couldn't help feeling that all this was just bullshit since I felt completely fine. Mum and I kept exchanging glances knowing that we weren't going to visit any one of those names suggested.

I was glad to turn my back to the hospital and couldn't wait to get home and on with my life.

Feeling just fine again, but still weakened we went to see Libby again. Libby had 'seen' that my aura was too open and therefore very vulnerable and referred me on to a lady that had psychic abilities and could help us in different ways. So we went to see her a week later and she told me that I was developing a 'gift', an ability to communicate with spirits and she gave me a few strategies on how to protect myself from being too open to unwanted entities. Even though mum and I gained a lot of insight, we both felt that something was missing. She did make a lot of sense and seemed to 'know' a lot, but some of it did not resonate with me nor my mum.

We felt that Libby was more insightful, beyond the 'metaphysical' and is all that is heart. Mum and I both somehow have a deep connection with her and trust her more than anyone.

Mum felt like I could gain from a 'mentor', since what we were dealing with wasn't something you could really talk to everyone about openly without being deemed weird or delusional.

Life resumed as normal as possible and I went back to school. It didn't take long though and I started having seizures again. Everyone was very concerned for me and my mum had to pick me up regularly. I missed a lot of school which I really didn't complain about.

In the meantime my mum met Donna. Donna is Max's mum. Max was a friend from earlier days at school since he left in Year 9 to move an hour out of Melbourne. Max took his own life only a few months prior to them meeting. I had been to Max's funeral in March with all my classmates.

Donna had told my mum that ever since Max had passed on, he was visiting her and she could communicate with him. He had told her that everything was going to be ok and he didn't realise how much he would hurt everyone by taking his own life. He used to be one of those children that just knew when someone was sad and in need of a hug. He also got bullied because of his perceptiveness and innate knowing.

I am just bringing this up here to show you that there are many things in life that can't be explained in what is considered 'normal' terms.

In July my mum and I visited her family back in Germany. My grandfather had turned blind overnight at the beginning of May for no apparent reason. My grandmother, who had onset of dementia, had to be admitted to a nursing home for the time being. We went over to spend some time to help him get accustomed to this new lifestyle.

On the way over to Germany, I had another seizure on the plane from Melbourne to Abu Dhabi. I wasn't prepared for all the energies coming in from the mass of people at the airport. Half way through the fifteen hour flight my legs began feeling numb and I realised that I was going to have a seizure. My mum could feel it too and asked the stewardess if they could lay me down on the floor. Some lady moved to make room for us in the exit area.

The stewardesses were very caring and one gentleman watching me was praying for me as I could somehow hear him – without actually 'hearing' him. I went up to him afterwards to thank him and he was puzzled as to how I knew about it.

Having come out of the seizure about forty-five minutes later, the stewardesses tried to convince me to take some drugs, they were worried, I was going to have another seizure and they kept on telling me that if I didn't and I would have another one, they would have to turn the plane around and it would become an insurance issue.

My mum comes from a well-established family near the Dutch border and my granddad's estate dates back around eight hundred years. He grew up in a castle which sadly was destroyed in the Second World War. The ruins of it are still existing and are bordering the farm house which was rebuilt after the war where he still lives to this day.

I felt a lot of unwanted presence in the old walls and we tried clearing the house to rid all the negative energies. This ticked off the negative spirits and we woke up with cuts and bruises all over our bodies – small but painful. My mum started shedding skin from her hands and feet.

I will talk more about negative energies, entities and clearing in a later chapter.

Spending much time alone in Germany as my mum was busy with my grandfather, I was happy doing my own thing and I felt free and extremely good within myself. I decided then to feel and be like this all the time and when I got back to Melbourne I planned telling my dad my decision to finally leave school for good.

Back at school I found myself having seizures every other day and my poor mum had to come and pick me up again and again and again. During class I began to have glimpses of peoples' situations at home, their struggles and lack of connection with their parents, feeling insecure around their friends and so much more. It overwhelmed me and I took on everyone's feelings which I had trouble dealing with.

My teachers were worried about me and my lack of attendance and asked us for a meeting. We decided then that I was going to do home schooling as I was presented with so many different options we had never even been told about. There are so many alternatives – and I am wondering why this is not openly shared?!

I ended up in hospital a few more times but as usual, nothing presented out of the ordinary as heart rhythm, blood, etc. were always all 'normal'. I was bombarded with everyone's take on things and everyone had their own opinion. Everyone believed that I was depressed and full of anxieties, not realizing that all the times I was fine – I really was fine!

At this time, Libby was my rock and she guided me through all things peculiar for a 'normal' person. She thought it wise that I talk to 'the man in the mountain' (as I like to refer to him) as he could give me a better understanding of what I was going through. Early August I had my first phone conversation with him for an hour. He was a very lovely man who knew things about me straight away and made me understand things easily. He went straight to the point and there was no bullshit. I trusted him instantly.

He explained that my body's convulsions were due to the release of past stored up energy. Apparently, all my past lives had been cut short and I had never lived past the age of around 20. I had lived through countless traumatic experiences still present in my current body. Some examples of those past lives were involving drug abuse, alcoholism, and suicide, another one was where I had been in a war and had been captured and then tortured until death.

These many extreme experiences had obviously a very traumatic effect on my soul and for some reason, those feelings were now coming up and out through my seizures.

Before we had the phone conversation, I was feeling very uneasy about life in general so I was vulnerable once again. That night I had yet another seizure but this time my whole body went limp from the intensity of the seizure. This was different from the other times.

I eventually fell asleep exhausted. As you can imagine, the next day, I had no energy and was incredibly fatigued, so I lay in bed all day. I spent countless hours by myself, all cooped up in my room. I began to really worry for my mental health. I was pondering everything that anyone had ever told me, so many voices, so many opinions, even my best friend wondered if I should get help and was questioning me – maybe I was crazy after all. I was confused and pretty rattled and felt at a complete loss. All my thoughts were drifting south, into the negative. I was aching all over, all this thinking and not knowing and too many people suggesting that I did have some mental issues – all this made me feel so hopeless.

I did not feel like myself, it was so dark in and around me.

I worried about the images that appeared in my head. Voices so loud, making me dig my fingers into my scalp. I was in so much pain. Something was definitely not right. Words spat out of my mouth uncontrollably, I could not make any sense of what I was saying. I was told to do things, bad things. Things that could make anyone tremble with fear. I was deeply troubled but had nowhere to escape.

That night I got out of bed eventually, not feeling like myself at all. I felt like I was being my own observer, making my way into the kitchen. I reached for the sharpest knife in the drawers and next thing I knew I was sitting on the cool lush grass of the golf course that is located just beyond our fence in our back yard. The cold metallic edge of the knife dug into my wrist. The voices grew louder and tears were rushing down my face. At this point I felt this pull and push within my body. It was almost as if I was fighting myself as another person. The force of this pull was so strong, my body was confused with the movements it was performing.

When all of a sudden there was this big rise of energy and then complete silence. Stumbling back into my house, wiping away my tears, I knocked on my mum's bedroom door. My dad was away on a business trip.

I stood frozen in the doorway and my mum awoke. She asked me if I was OK. Later she told me that I kept repeating: "Please don't be angry", and "I am so sorry", over and over again. Then I yelled out 'my arm' through my tears.

My mum at the time thought I had been dreaming and was in a state where I believed I was in one of my past lives from the day before and lost my arm. I then collapsed on the floor and my mum picked me up to walk me into my bedroom constantly reassuring me that she wasn't angry but concerned. She lay next to me and held me tight. I kept on repeating myself: "please don't be angry", and "I am so sorry".

The pain that was running through my body and my wrist made me scream out: "You are not listening to me", "you never listen to me".

My mum just held me and kept comforting me until she couldn't take it any longer and made me show my arms to reassure me that nothing was wrong. That's when she saw the cut on my left wrist. It wasn't a deep cut but worrying nevertheless.

My mum screamed out for my older sister who came running and got some bandages. They dressed my wound and I fell asleep not long after in the comfort of my mum's arms.

Waking up the next morning, I found my wrist in the bandage and it took me awhile to remember what had happened the night before. My stomach turned and I felt sick. I had never before felt so much discomfort in my body and so much fear of what I was able to do.

The feeling of embarrassment and shame washed over me and shook my whole body. I felt so embarrassed because of my mother.

I love my mother dearly and respect her with all my heart. Whilst fighting the voices and negative entities, thinking of her gave me the strength not to go all the way that night.

You see, my mother has a very strong and beautiful way about her that she sees people for their full potential and helps them flourish to meet their own highest expectations. My mother has given me so much nurturing and supported me always in pursuing my dreams that I thought it would be selfish to take my own life. I couldn't face the pain she would be in if I would have done the unthinkable.

Having someone in your life that you look up to and respect is vital for self-acceptance and makes you think about your responsibilities towards that person and others. Having that guidance and nurturing in your life helps you excel and reach your goals and most importantly excel in your well-being. I feel that there is such a lack of good parenting and role modelling in today's world.

Mum and I never told my dad about it as it was too scary and as my mum said to me in the car; "If you do it once, it will never happen again. If you do it twice, it will happen again."

Other than that, my life was at a high. Every time I came out of one of my seizures I saw everything much clearer and my senses seemed heightened. I gained a deeper understanding of my environment and the people in it. I began to unlock different aspects of my potential and the ME I never knew I was and had inside of me.

I read a lot about supernatural occurrences and the magical and I realised that there are so many people sharing similar experiences and that they were nothing like being portrayed in movies. Every experience is a different one for everyone and so hard to put into words and explain to an outsider without freaking them out or thinking of you as a bit loopy.

I understood that something magical was in my blood and that everything I studied felt more like a remembering. All my experiences were completely normal to me and somehow I knew that I was on a journey and had to go through these challenging times to grow.

Even though September and October were very dark months, they were my most important time for my transition. During that time I was pushed to the limits and was played with by negative entities that were controlling my body. They were trying to keep me back from becoming my true self and to develop my powers.

Throughout that time, I would catch myself saying really bizarre things that sounded like ancient languages. I would find myself being exceedingly offensive and expressing myself with complete arrogance. When one night a heated argument boiled up in the kitchen. My head filled with such rage. Images rushed into my head, and made me cringe by the thought of their existence. At that point I knew I had to get out, before I did something harmful.

I ended up sitting on a park bench yelling at myself when people started to stare. I remember mumbling with fear "why are you in me" and telling them to "get out." Hearing my own words, I was so very frightened but at the same time felt relief. My mum had been driving around worried for me and found me and drove me back home.

She asked me what the hell was the matter with me and I began to hysterically scream from this pain that sprouted in my body. We walked inside the house and mum held me tight and told me repeatedly that she loved me and that all was good. Then out of nowhere I collapsed within her arms. She panicked but then within an instance I regained full control of my body and the negative entity had left. I was exhausted but felt like me again.

Within that time we made several trips to see the 'man in the mountains', as I like to refer to him as. He brought much clarity into my life and really helped me with managing and controlling my seizures.

He explained that something amazing was happening to me. He said I was experiencing "a Kundalini awakening", an arising of pure energy and consciousness. Surprisingly I was going through this all naturally, making me feel kind of special and honoured whereas other people had to go through many years of spiritual training to achieve such enlightenment.

He told me that at this point I was half way through with peeling back the layers of past experiences that had manifested in my body. My seizures were making room for a 'bigger' engine to cope with what was to come.

"When Kundalini energy
activates,
it offers an opportunity for the
complete transformation of your life.
It will support you in your
deepest longing
for Truth and Self-Realisation,
if you will only surrender and
trust the process."

-

Bonnie Greenwell Ph.D.

In order for my body to accelerate this process my body had to be tuned to a different frequency and a surge of higher voltage was needed to clear my body from all negative attachments and embodiments.

Kundalini awakening can trigger a wide range of phenomena, both positive and negative. It can change in the physical, emotional, sensate and psychic capacities, cause stress in vulnerable areas of the body, open the heart and mind to major shifts in perspective, and cause many unique and unfamiliar sensations including shaking, vibrating, spontaneous movement, visions, and many other occurrences.

In my particular case the seizures were my expression of it.

For more in-depth information I would suggest to read more about it and form your own opinion as this is something many people do not talk about.

It felt good to be reassured that I wasn't going crazy. Being a teenager and feeling more than the average person finds you in a position often of despair as you have trouble relating to your peers and all that is wrong in the world.

I was gaining knowledge and my long-term memory was returning and I gained a deeper understanding looking through the eyes of a child – the way we are supposed to look at the world – in wonder and awe. Being one with all and all with one. My tolerance level for things that just don't make sense was decreasing also.

∞

I was helping my mum cleaning the house all morning and later on for lunch met up with my cousin for a bite to eat. Afterwards I quickly picked up some clothes from my friend and had to leave her since my left ear was aching and caused me much discomfort.

Arriving home all I was able to do was curl up on my bed as the pain grew stronger and stronger. It was unbearable. The pain travelled down along my jaws and I thought my head was going to explode. I curled up in a foetal position and cried from the sheer intensity.

Mum gave me a hot water bottle but I refused everything, this was the worst pain I had ever experienced. I didn't want to be touched nor spoken to and eventually screamed out for help, for 'someone' to help me. I needed help! Mum had already called the local doctor but I went down rapidly. My dad arrived home just in time to carry me out to the car as I had collapsed in my mum's arms while she was trying to walk me to get ready to leave for the doctors. I had simply shut down and gone to sleep. My body was totally limp.

My parents then took me to the closest medical centre and was seen by the doctor on duty. My body wasn't responding at all, there was no resistance and I felt like being not part of my body at the same time in it but unable to control it.

This was one of the most terrifying moments for my parents. My mum was scared to lose me that evening and even the doctor was too alarmed so he called for an ambulance to have me taken straight to hospital.

I felt like going through some sort of transitioning – you know when you try and download something from the computer and the clock counts down until ready – it was strangely calming until I felt a sharp pain in my thumb (it was either that or they were going to put a tube down my throat to help me breathe), then I heard myself hissing; "*You f***ing wa*Ker*".

Where the hell did that come from? I would never even dare to say those words out loud to anyone and there they were – very clear!

They strapped me to the stretcher and I was hyperventilating, my hands were all tensed up and looked like I had really bad arthritis, I could not feel nor move my body.

I overheard the paramedic, who had hurt me earlier, blame my mother for encouraging me. What absolute BS! She asked him to just let me be, to do what I had to. How, though, would he understand what I was going through and what my mum knew so well and was only trying to support me.

Arriving at the hospital I was already cracking jokes with my dad and feeling very much myself again. As always I was free to go fairly quickly as nothing came up on any monitor.

The following days I felt weak and needed a lot of sleep. At one point I saw white light everywhere and I could not help but cry.

It seemed that everything I did, was in extremes. I had my period for over 8 weeks and that particular afternoon, when we were at a family gathering, I felt very faint. I was losing so much blood and we had to leave for home. We ended up AGAIN in hospital. This time we went to a private one as my mum could not deal with the public system any longer. Too many hospital visits, too much waiting in the queue, too little attention. When we arrived in the evening we were the only ones there and everybody was so lovely and caring.

One of the male nurses cracked me up as he was joking around with me a lot. And then it was my turn to make him laugh hysterically telling him that I was taking tree bark in brandy as medication … my only form of treatment.

I was put on a drip and they replaced some fluid and salts and I felt better in no time. Oh, just before we got to hospital, I started convulsing again but stopped within the first minutes we arrived.

I was learning to control my seizures.

I also refused taking any other 'drugs' that were prescribed as they were playing with my mind and didn't do anything to help.

My parents had flown to Hong Kong for business which left my two sisters and I at home. During the days I was very lethargic, staying in bed all day. I felt unable to move much and my entire body was aching. My legs went numb and a tingling sensation generated throughout my body. The abnormality of this made the sensation extremely uncomfortable to handle.

A powerful thrust came from my chest and I was having another seizure. For someone to be viewing what was happening it would have looked like something from a possessive horror movie. The voices were yelling at me and made it just that much harder to cope with. I yelled out with force to try and release some pressure that was accumulating in my head. My sister Maddie came running into my room and was trying to remain calm but watching me convulsing rather severely and moving about my bed frantically, it was hard to not be frightened. She was shaking and really worried for me.

I tried telling her to take me to the hospital but I only could manage murmuring. It took a while for her to understand me and she immediately rang the ambulance in a frenzy.

When I am in this state it is exceedingly difficult to talk. It's as if my brain shuts down and forgets how to speak. It feels like I am at a still point and forgot how to even think. Everything is a struggle.

Maddie then rang my parents overseas with panic in her heart. My parents organised for our friend and neighbour, Petrina to come and be with us.

When the ambulance arrived my body was still jolting. And since my room is in the back of the house, in order to get the stretcher through, the paramedics had to come through the back door.

And guess what?! The same paramedic who had hurt my thumb to bring me back the last time, was here yet again. My heart sank a little. Ok, I'm not gonna lie – a lot.

They proceeded with their standard tests for heart rate, blood pressure, eye movements, etc. – but yet again, there was nothing physically wrong with me. I was taken into the ambulance and another paramedic asked me questions about what I was experiencing. I told him that I was hearing voices – bad idea – because now he suggested that I was probably schizophrenic reassuring me that there were good drugs out there now, that wouldn't even make me feel sick, like the once before – what a winner!

I didn't feel like being Me at this time at all again. I had no feelings, no thoughts.

Back at the hospital, Petrina and my sisters had followed the ambulance in her car and were sitting with me, a doctor came in and wanted to talk to me alone. He began to ask me the usual questions about depression and anxiety. I did tell him that I had already been diagnosed with both.

I also told him about the voices in my head telling me to do things I had no influence over as my body felt hijacked at times by these negative forces.

I found myself also going back to the time when I was bullied and ended up crying uncontrollably. The doctor left and came back 10 minutes later.

He said to me (something along the lines of the following); "You have schizophrenia and/or bipolar disorder. You will be emitted into Melbourne clinic and they will assess you and keep you under surveillance for 2 weeks. You need to address your issues."

Some part of me was grateful for the diagnosis as I had now confirmation that there was something really not right with me.

Again, as physically everything was OK, Petrina drove us all back home and she treated us for dinner. Usually I came out of the seizures with a deeper knowing and happy. This time though, I stayed in the negative and felt dead inside. My sister organised friends to come around to comfort and spend time with me for some well needed distraction for all of us.

Some of our friends were sitting outside while I stayed in with my friend, Lachie as I confided in him. I told him about all the things that had happened and what the doctors had told me. Lachie knew me to be different, happy and quirky but not to be depressive or negative. He listened intently to all I had to say and comforted me with reassurance that all would be fine. He did not believe that I had schizophrenia nor any of the other diagnosed issues.

At one point before this episode, I did look up about schizophrenia on the internet and I found a list with symptoms. I was doing a sort of test where I ticked all the boxes.

It read: "the main symptoms of schizophrenia are hallucinations meaning believing something that isn't real, such as hearing voices when no one is there… unusual behaviour…confused thoughts."

I talk to spirits all the time and hear voices on a regular basis. This does not make me crazy. I am very much a so called "normal" girl when it comes to playing in the human world.

∞

I had discussed this with my mum and we were agreeing how quickly someone could come to believe being or having a condition purely by ticking certain boxes. She advised me not to consult Dr. Google.

Completely exhausted and still not feeling much, I went to sleep and my sister, Maddie stayed with me throughout the night.

My mum was flying back from Hong Kong overnight and arrived late morning to find me and my sisters still asleep. The previous day had taken a toll on all of us.

She recalls that when she came to see me, she felt somehow strange looking at me and not feeling me. It wasn't her daughter laying there. She was scared for me and what was happening.

She let me sleep and got busy around the house. I woke up much later and felt terrible, I wasn't saying much and my head was aching with noise. It was hurting so much and I needed to hold my head so that it wouldn't explode.

I was lethargic and walked around the house aimlessly. My hands started contorting from the pressure I felt inside trying to release the tension.

My mum has now tried for a while to talk with me to see where I am at, but I don't want to talk, don't want to listen. I end up rocking back and forth all hunched over sitting on the front porch hiding under my hoody. My mum has serious worries about my state and wants to talk desperately.

I don't respond and finally I tell her to go away. I tell her to stop talking and that she was making me angry. And what did she do? She got me even more and more angry by forcing the issue and telling me to feel what I was feeling and even telling me to be angry. She pushed me so hard that I almost lost it, I wanted to hurt her. She told me to face my fears and that I had a choice. A choice of fighting whatever THIS was or giving into it.

I didn't want to hear it.

She grabbed me and tried looking at me but I was fighting her and that's when I needed to get away. I was in a frantic state and wanted to run into my room and out to the golf course to be free of what I was feeling. My mum pursued me into my room, now seriously scared and stopped me from running out my back door. That's when it came over me again and I started convulsing. We both ended up on the floor as I was struggling to get her off me, but she held on tight and there was no escaping. It went on for a while until my sister, Maddie called the ambulance again. It was too much to just stand by and observe even though my mum thought she had it under control. I had developed such strength that my mum and my sister had to hold me down so I wouldn't hurt myself.

Within no time, a paramedic appeared and by that time I was already coming out of it. He spoke to my mum and asked, since she seemed to have me under control and I had calmed down, to have a chat with my sisters. He wanted to know about the family situation and ensure, that I wasn't abused or something else was going on.

He came back and sat with me, asking me so many questions. He told me that he thought that is was OK to stay here as my mum seemed to know how to handle the situation but also gave me the option of coming with the ambulance to the hospital.

I wanted to go to hospital.

I wanted to get away, away from everyone and everything.

I didn't want to deal with anything or anyone.

My mum had to swallow hard but ensured me that whatever my decision, she would be right behind me.

Whatever I needed, she just wanted me to be happy, most of all, safe. She wanted her daughter back. She felt the disconnection since I wasn't really me.

Two more paramedics did the routine checks on me and then took me back to hospital.

My sister, Maddie, who had been my rock throughout those past days was going through VCE at the same time and had exams the following day. My mum dropped her off to our friend, Petrina's house so she could get some rest and try to do some last minute work.

My older sister, Sophia accompanied me in the ambulance and stayed with me in my allocated room until my mum appeared. She recalls that she still felt this distance between us and that this was not her daughter sitting there. I kept hiding under my hoody and only gave abrupt answers to her questions how I was feeling.

My mum and Sophia were asked to leave the room as 2 ladies from the Psych-ward wanted to assess me. One was a blond lady in her 40s and the other a lady in a similar age from New Zealand with dreadlocks and tattoos on her face above and under her lips. Those tattoos are called 'ta moko"– each moko contains ancestral tribal messages specific to the wearer. These messages tell the story of the wearer's family and tribal affiliation, and their place in these social structures. A moko's message also portrays the wearer's genealogy, knowledge and social standing.

Apparently, when the ladies had passed my mum and sister on their way out, my mum just took one look at the Maori lady and full of judgement whispered to my sister; 'look at her, now she is going to tell me that my daughter is crazy, what does she know?', my mum was very suspicious. Sophia turned to her and told her to be quiet and to put herself together and to stop judging. "You don't know this lady, how dare you judge her like that?!"

The ladies sat down with me and asked me more questions. I told them everything that had happened including that I had tried to harm myself. I told them about the voices and communicating with spirits.

The Maori lady then told me about her grandma also communicating with spirits and that this had a long tradition in her family. Hearing that other people did do the same and that it wasn't weird or crazy, I suddenly regained my energy and full consciousness and the negative entity left me abruptly. I was totally me again.

The 2 asked me to wait as they wanted to have a chat with mum. They left and I just sat on the bed – completely drained and realising what I had put everyone through.

So this is what happened then; the ladies went to have a chat with my mum and Sophia. They asked what my mum was making of it all, as they did not think that there was anything wrong with me other than that I was a lovely teenager. My mum, sick and tired of all the labelling and suggestions from former doctors, the secrecy about what I was really going through, just said to them: "let's just cut through the bull shit". And told them everything that we had been through for the past year and beyond. She didn't care anymore what anyone was making of all of this. She spoke about changes in the world she was observing and how especially the young ones were being affected by those changes, that children were more vulnerable now due to more and more negative influences, over-stimulation through technology, a growing disconnect of people, the lack of leadership on a global scale and so much more. The ladies agreed on everything that poured out of her and it all ended in tears as they were hugging each other tightly assuring each other that I was OK and that I was blessed to be developing a gift (or whatever you want to call it).

They told my mum that they couldn't write any of that 'stuff' into their report, but they did 'see' what was happening and they were very happy to 'clear' me of any labels all the other doctors had tried to place on me.

My mum had one last request before they left. She asked the ladies to go and tell me all that they had told my mum and that they also thought that something was evolving within me that was acceptable in some cultures or beliefs. Mum wanted to ensure that I knew that she wasn't the only person believing in my transitioning. I had to understand that what the 'man in the mountains' had already told me and was coaching and mentoring me through was real. I shouldn't doubt ever again and trust in my intuitions, never to question again that something was wrong with me.

The ladies came back into my room and I felt appalled with myself again that I hadn't been strong enough to fight off the negative, that it had to come to this. They said to me: "You are an amazing girl and you should be so lucky and embrace your extraordinary gift! There is nothing wrong with you and we wish you best of luck on your journey."

We said our good-byes and then we were ready to leave. I was so eager to get out of there. My mum could 'feel' Me again, I apologised to her over and over again for what I had done, and she just gave me the biggest hug and was so happy that she had her daughter back.

I had a big rest at home and slept what seemed forever. I felt so good afterwards, except from the lingering feeling of disappointment and embarrassment.

A couple of days later I was looking out of my window and saw the most beautiful light in the garden and it came with a feeling of abundance of happiness and everything and anything positive and an overpowering emotion of bliss. It felt like a gateway to an amazing future ahead.

Nevertheless, I did experience jolts from time to time but I was able to control them now. I would feel them coming on and simply saw myself fully protected with a deeper knowledge of my incredible journey. I was accepting what I was going through completely and took full responsibility.

I was changing. I opened my ability to see things for what they are on an all different level. I was tapping into different sources of information, whether it was from people or my environment. Going to places with masses of people, like shopping malls or markets, I feel tired and exhausted, actually completely worn out within next to no time. It seems like that people 'suck' my energy right out of me. My body starts pulsating, I get a headache and my legs start feeling numb – that's my queue to get out of there.

I have learned to 'clear' myself from all the energies that I take on board. I know now when to leave certain places and when not to go out. My feelings are never wrong and I need a lot of time to myself.

Don't get me wrong, I love socialising and spending time with family and friends. Having a good night out, singing, dancing brings me so much joy, but then I need a lot of time to recharge my batteries. During that time on my own, I learn so much from all that I am given. I feel utterly at peace, a happiness that is beyond influences from outside of me. All of the power comes from the core of my being and I feel so connected to all that surrounds me, I feel one with everyone and everything and draw my energy from that.

I have yet a while to go as my journey continues and I know that life will throw challenges my way that I can't fathom yet, but I know they are coming in a way that I need to experience them as and I am accepting of it. Everything has a positive impact on my inner growth, the person I am becoming even though it might be looked upon as negative. For me it is always only right for me. I am sovereign, I am free and no one can own me.

I no longer listen to people's opinions and judgements as I know that this is my very own journey and I know who I am. There is no wonder pill, not any medication that will address what I needed to find out for myself, for that I am almighty and all powerful on my own accord. There is no place for a 'band-aid', if you want to mend your soul – the marvellous You.

I know that every single person has it in them to be their own true self and this is my appeal to You 'to soar and fly high'.

Part 2

The Universal Laws

Although there are many laws governing the universe, I would first like to touch base on this particular one, **the law of attraction**, as I have done most of my research surrounding this area.

Simply put, the law of attraction is the ability to attract anything into your life whatever you are focusing on. This law uses the power of your mind to translate your thoughts and driving it into reality.

Everything is Energy.
I am not a scientist, but I now fully understand it. "Science, through Quantum Physics, is showing us that everything in our universe is energy".
The book you are holding is made up of energy, the chair you're sitting on, your body - everything is energy.

Everything vibrates.
Everyone and everything has their own vibrational frequency. The Law of Vibration is known as 'nothing rests'.
What people don't really know is, that a simple thought also transmits a vibrational frequency - resulting in the magnet effect; that by sending out a certain vibrational frequency, it has to link up to a

form of reality.

For example, you keep picturing your dream car and next thing you know you're seeing that type of car all over town. Or if you're thinking of someone you haven't spoken to in a while and then out of nowhere, they ring you or bump into them on the street. This is the result of the power of thought.

You see, thought is one of the most powerful tools you have.

On the flip-side of the coin, if you are endlessly thinking about how your life is a mess, how everything bad always happens to you, how you're unlucky, you're this, you're that - all the same neighbouring negative thoughts, you are requesting the universe to do just that.
And the universe does not disappoint! Ever!

Next thing you know, you lose your job, you have to sell the house, your car breaks down and your phone dies. It's like the domino effect.

You're sending out a negative vibration into the universe and your delivery has been very much accounted for.
You might be thinking, I don't want to be in those situations, I haven't been asking for this!?

Well, what you are doing is thinking of what you do **not** want. That alone is a thought, right? So what you have to do is visualise what you **do** want and only that.

Instead of saying "I don't want to be late on the payment of my bills again", you could say, "I'm so happy my bills were paid on time."

Shifting your thought process will be quite a task in the beginning but once you practise it, it becomes easier every day. It's just like riding a bike.

Practice makes perfect.

In order for the Universe to respond to your wishes in a way you want, you have to stay in the positive, never allowing a negative thought. This is of utmost importance. That's why I get very annoyed with the negative messages on our roads with signs like "Speed kills" sending the wrong message altogether. Because all you will then be focusing on is the killing bit. It should rather read: "Slow down, someone at home loves you!"

So just make sure that you are very specific about what you ask for. And be positive. Ask for what you DO want and not what you DON'T want.

Ways that can help you guarantee success:
- Write down what you want, your dreams and desires. For example, a new home, job, family,

deep relationships, wealth, success, happiness, whatever it may be. This will vary for everyone.

- Place it where you are most certain to see it, e.g. on your bed frame or a mirror, maybe in the toilet, somewhere it's visible and will be seen more than three times a day.
- Take five minutes to view what you wrote and indulge in an all-embracing visualisation method:

  1. Close your eyes.
  2. Take three deep and long breaths to get into an alpha state (a more relaxed state of mind).
  3. Go back to a time where you felt absolute happiness and fully embrace the moment as if you were experiencing it once again. Imagine that you already have it. Placing your contemplations into existence by tricking your subconscious into thinking you already have it, creates confusion to the universe and speeds up the process of having it in the reality formation. Whatever that might be.
     Make sure that your feeling is matching your desire and that this feeling is real. This is the most important and essential prerequisite to bring anything you want into manifestation.
  4. Say thank you at the end of the visualisation practise.

Preferably, do this 3x a day or as many times as you can.

Being grateful for already having what you want, you are emitting that frequency of already having what you want in your life. When this happens the universe is puzzled as to why you don't have it already, this generating a higher rate towards the outcome/end result.

The stronger positive emotions are being brought into your wish, the greater the force to make your wish a reality.

Since positive emotions like love, gratitude and joy are resonating at a very high frequency, the result is sure to be created faster.
Negative emotions, on the other hand, like judgment, anger and hate are vibrating on a lower frequency.
So Positive emotions will always overrule negative ones.

A little mention here though, never be fooled by the power of negativity. It can do much harm so it all lies within you on what you choose to focus your attention on.

I would like you to have a think about your current situation. Are you happy about how your life, are your friends supportive and good for you, is your intimate relationship one of balance and pure love? Are you happy with your job or your current income??

If your answers are all yes, then great - keep on doing what you're doing! But if you are not happy with even one of those, all you have to do is shift your focus. Start to conceive your true needs and wants and be adamant about it.

Everything in your life right now, including the things you're complaining about, you have somehow attracted. For many, this will be hard to accept.

By accepting this fact though, you are one step closer to taking responsibility for your situation. There is no shame in this, unless you don't do anything about it and keep complaining.

Correlating with the Law of attraction is the power of belief.

Your belief is like a thought and is also emanating a certain frequency.

"Believe and you shall receive"

-

Matthew 21:22

Believing that you are 'lucky', you send out the appropriate signal. Your belief, like any religion, shapes your reality.

Religion is purely based on your belief system. If you believe in what you have been brought up to believe to be true, you will follow what you have learned.

Every religion is 'learned' from your environment and your immediate influences. So every religion is right, because it helps you in certain ways, yet also wrong as you then separate yourself from others following another religion. In conclusion, religion is simply another form of identification and belonging.

Depending which country you are born in, which faith your family is following, you will grow up with what your parents will have taught you.

Just as you don't get born to hate, you learn to believe that your religion is the one and only, the right one.

So where does that leave the one that does not follow your religion/your belief?

Every religion has its own right but it doesn't make it necessarily THE RIGHT ONE!

We all believe in something, even if we say that we don't believe in anything – that is still a belief though. Whatever works for you, even if you take some of this and some of that, if you can mix and match to your own conviction, why not take the best of everything?! As long as it works for you and you don't go around having to convince anyone that you are the only one with the right belief.

Personally, I have done the same. I have read about many teachings and keep doing it, but mostly I trust my intuition and pick and choose anything that correlates with my very own belief but mostly what feels right to me.

"In reality,
there are as many religions
as there are individuals."

-

Mahatma Ghandi

Appreciation and Gratitude

"Imagine the world we could live in once we appreciate the privilege of life"

To be happy every day, showing appreciation and gratitude is by far the most important approach. It is even scientifically proven that one of the supreme contributing influences to overall happiness in your life is how much gratitude you show. By recognising even the smallest thing to be grateful for, you habitually regulate your thinking into the now.

We are always looking to the future, always waiting for the next opportunity, the next time, to make IT happen, whatever that might be. Only ever living in the future is dismissing the moment – and this moment is the only time that is real – the now is the only time you really have.

Going through what I have been now for the past year, I've figured out the secret of my own happiness. Appreciation for everything you've got - whether it's a little or a lot.

With concentrating on now and appreciating everything you have now, you heighten your potential happiness. Once you begin to do so, you will see an instant shift in your life's experience. There is always something to be appreciative and grateful for.

Showing gratitude is also an instant connection to your heart.

The brain thinks, but the heart knows.

-

Dr. Joe Dispenza

Being consistent in your practice of appreciation you're transmitting one of the highest energy vibrations into the universe, as well as raising your own personal energy field.

Being happy in your current situation, magnetises more happiness within your day to day life.

"The more grateful you are, The more you have to be grateful for"

Self Love

Self-love is exceedingly one of the most important things for a child to learn.

It wouldn't even hurt anyone else to do the same. Despite your circumstances or environment, if you can learn to love yourself, you will help yourself being able to face many challenges in the future.

Too many people, especially teens, are having trouble with the acceptance of who they are and loving themselves. It is a struggle to be comfortable within their own skin. What happens here is when you don't fully accept who you are and thrive on your uniqueness and what you have to offer, no one can actually love you if it can't be reflected by your own feelings.

We mirror everything we say and do.

Your own restrictive belief sets limitations for someone else to love you full heartedly, as you are only able to see and expect as much love from the other as you see from within yourself.

When you learn to love yourself, you begin to feel whole. People ask 'How do I love myself, if I hate who

I am and what I look like?'
Well, first you must learn to accept yourself.

Acceptance is key. No matter how hard it is in the beginning, you have to let go and just be acceptant.

'Fake it till you make it', like my mum always says. Once you keep telling yourself that you are lovable, loving and beautiful, which you truly are, you accept yourself as that and you will learn to love yourself.

How did you come to believe that you are anything less than perfect?

You are working with your subconscious and you are creating a normality within your thinking - all the while tricking your subconscious.
It obviously helps a lot if you act upon your thoughts.

Once you have learnt to accept yourself as you are, the next step is to see yourself as what you truly desire to be, as if you are already that person. If it's a confident and aspiring person, tell yourself this every day and practise until you achieve your desired state.
Again, learn to FEEL more and into what you want.

There is a major absence of self-love in the world.

The lack of love from your immediate environment

is hurtful and leaves you empty and sad. Sometimes people are unable to love you, because they don't love themselves.

This should not stop you from loving yourself though, nor keep you from learning to love yourself. You can draw love from anything living, eg. a tree, an animal or even one of your 'imaginary' friends. You can find the necessary power within, not having to wait for the outside to show you love. If you can take initiative to love yourself, no matter your circumstance or situation, you will succeed.

Self-love opens many doors to great experiences and situations. When you begin to love yourself you are playing your exclusive and very unique role on this planet.

<blockquote>

"If you're searching
for that
one person
that will change
your life,
take a look in the mirror."

</blockquote>

Limitations

It's not who you are
that holds you back,
It's who you think
you are not.

-

Denis Waitley

All throughout life we are subconsciously being fed
limited beliefs, someone else's limited beliefs.

Our parents bestow on us what they have learned
or have come to believe. We are all a product of our
environment at first, our direct influences. We come to
believe someone else's truth.

Since it is someone else's belief, it will always only
be that until we find our own – if we ever do.

We develop a certain mindset over time; your mind
is SET on what you have come to believe. This usually
happens through someone exercising some sort of
power over you, be it by force or coercion. Some
parents are very good with 'making you feel real bad' if
you don't do something the way they expect from you.
They work you by means of guilt.

If – then!!

What we children need though is true leadership, someone that sees pure potentiality in us, lifts our spirits to soar and believes in anything being possible at the same time keeping us safe and secure and loving us unconditionally.

Holding on to our lives being limited confines us in this small box of thinking that there are no real opportunities and that you have to make do with what is being given to you or what other people tell you is possible.
Too many people tell you what you can't and shouldn't be doing, rather than being encouraging and supportive.

Know that there are No Limitations as you are the only one that will make things happen or not. Whatever you think is possible, will be so when you truly open up for it and believe in it.

Many people have lost their imagination and are stuck in the past, often someone else's past.

Imagination can take you out of this SET belief. Relying on your imagination and to believe in the possibilities will take you to a 'road less travelled'.

This means you need to try and let things go a little, and start taking yourself less serious. Have fun being the new you and just be open to it all. Take complete charge of your life and own that you create your own reality. Don't hold back and place any restrictions on your thoughts – live YOUR life.

With imagination you can break through anything and we can BE anything we want to be. Facing our fears head on and believing in our dreams will set us free!! This will allow ourselves to live our lives beyond our 'imaginary' limitations.

"Borders are
where the actual ends but
also where imagination
and your story begins.

Challenge yourself to look at your
limitations as blessings,
not as stopping blocks."

-

Amy Purdy: Living beyond limits

Entity Attachments

OK, I know what you are thinking now – this is going a bit far. But just have a read and keep an open mind.

Many people, but mostly children, can see spirits or another way to put it, they 'talk to the dead' or 'hear voices'.

Spirits come to a person in a form that is familiar and recognisable to them. For each person it is a very different experience.

Some can see spirits but can't communicate with them, others can. Then there are others that feel spirits and/or their energy, some even smell or simply know of their existence, some even see colours. Because we are individuals, it is very different for every single one of us.

For every one of us who is actually having an experience of that sort, it is hard to transmit to others the magnitude and depth of our experience, making it lose its core value and profoundness once spoken about.

Personally, I don't like to talk about my experiences

to people because of their judgements and as it gets thrown out of context.

But I believe it's important to share some of my interactions with spirits, in order to create a normalisation upon having this ability.

Maybe you have felt a presence, saw something at the corner of your eye or wondered why you have thought or said something that is totally out of character.

Maybe you should be doing things that you know you have to do, or address or change something about yourself, but just don't seem to ever get there or find any energy for it. Maybe you feel numb and disorientated, confused and a bit hopeless, this could simply be an attachment that is zapping you of your quintessential life force. The force that drives you as a perfect created human being and allows you to experience happiness and bliss.

Just be open to knowing that there is something beyond what you have been told. Because, after all, who is stopping you but yourself.

There is no need to be 'scared' either as you are the only one in charge. Nothing can happen to you unless you somehow agree to it, consciously or unconsciously.

In early 2016 my ability to communicate with spirits

developed. I was visited by many spirits and angels, not in the common understanding of angels, more like helpers.

They played a huge significant role concerning my capability to stay grounded* on this earth plane.

What I later discovered was that negative entities can high-jack your body and make you do things that seem unfamiliar to your reality. Note, that these entities are actually NOT allowed to do this without your permission. So if you ever experience this just deny access and they must leave you. Again, it's always you who is ultimately in charge.

People only experience these types of occurrences when they are vulnerable, feeling depressed, or shameful. There is also a heightened influence whilst you're asleep. The negative entities like to play tricks on you and being asleep you are an easy target. Again, denying access or praying for divine protection will help you.

Here are a few examples of the influence from Negative entities:

- Depression and anxiety
- Sudden change in personality
- Addictions
- Strange Behaviour or use of words
- Violent behaviour without remorse
- Continuous negative thoughts including

suicide.
- Physical pain and symptoms that can't heal
- Nightmares, terrors

These are often misunderstood occurrences and misinterpreted as illnesses of the body only.

When I went through the unsettling times of not knowing what was happening with me and having been bombarded with so many different opinions from so-called experts, I was lucky enough to have found people that see a bigger picture and were completely supportive and positive, believing in me and my purity. They never allowed me to view myself anything less than perfect.

Materialistic Society

Sadly, what seems to be happening in the world today, is that we judge each other for what we have and not for who we are or what we could be.

In a world run by materialistic values we forget that true happiness lies in our relationship to ourselves and others.

We have our lives dictated by so called 'experts', thus we shy away from our own true innate power and wisdom. We are no longer trusting our instincts and deeper knowledge from the abundant well deep inside of each and every one of us.

Jealousy and greed and needing to 'keep it up with the Joneses' alienates us from our true need for connection.

It's no longer about sharing and caring, it's all about holding on and to get ahead.

But when natural disasters occur and in time of suffering, people pull together and start helping each other. They follow their pure heart and their natural instincts. All barriers seem to be breaking down and we simply act without thinking. This feeling defeats all greed, competition and a feeling of separation.

Why are we waiting for a natural disaster to occur to live like decent humans? It sure says something about the influence of materialistic thinking; we forget out natural role we should play on this earth as a part of a bigger picture, part of a whole not being or feeling superior to anything or anyone.

Anything you own, can be destroyed or taken away at any time. The more we have, the more we want. We never seem satisfied. Or do we?

We are being bombarded with enticing messages telling us what we should have and ask for and expect. Everyone always seems to know what we want and need. Billboards, marketing slogans, advertising are sending all these subliminal messages to our brains and we allow them to manifest deep inside of us.

But we do have choices, we only have stopped taking a minute to think and re-consider and allow our own thoughts to prevail.

People say that money does not make one happy, but we all chase it and think that the illusion of money, which is only really a piece of paper or a coin made of metal will buy us at least a piece of happiness. The value of money changes all the time and is dependent on people's perception of it and what others tell us its worth.

We don't realise that we can't eat money, breathe

money, nor buy ourselves happiness – which we all are in desperate need of.

The true currency is our feeling of happiness.

Moments and memories will stay with us forever but a designer chair or the latest crave or brand product won't last and will quickly fade into the mundane – we already are looking for the next acquisition.

Of course we want to manifest materialistic things as we live in a materialistic world, but know that the true source of happiness lies within you and the people you are surrounding yourself with.

Make good choices and be responsible for your actions and be considerate and respectful to your environment, be it people or places.

False Consciousness

Our society is tuned into a very low vibrational frequency set by governments and the media.

It's as if false underlying intentions have been lodged within the human consciousness that are pulling masses of people into an unnatural matrix of false consciousness, leading towards self-destruction, which I refer to as the 'Vibrational Illusion'.

This results in blindness and ignorance to the truth, not being able to realise our own innate capabilities and true powers.

This perverted state of mind stops people from seeking to improve their lives. If only everyone would get together and demand a better life for everyone and not just an elite few!

It seems that people have taken on a set of beliefs that they have no power to question the status quo and act upon it.

Where are the revolutionaries to ask for things to make sense again and to question all the things that are not right but rotten?!

Manipulation

People who believe that they play a higher, more important role in life compared to others and have power over people seem to limit us to an extent to reach our full potential. Little do we realise, that we are always in charge and can make our own decisions who and what to accept and whether to question authority and/or the status quo.

I believe that big companies and governments are very well aware of this. Even Adolf Hitler wrote in his book "Mein Kampf" about how he used the laws of Suggestion to manipulate the people resulting in his successful ruling as a leader.

Unconsciously, we are surrounding ourselves with limitations thus not perceiving them as so. For example, at school, you might be given an assignment having to consider the following; 600 words, analytical essay, structured paragraphs. This being a set task, it has perimeters that you have to work with.

There will be a certain percentage that will excel in this area, but if you ask students to explore something that they are passionate about, then their creative juices will flow with ease and this will create an opening for their real talents and ingenuity.

Being given a task there is always an element of limitation due to its inherent structure which is not necessarily a bad thing. I am just pointing out that over time this will keep adding very subtly yet powerfully to an acceptance of restrictions. Just like laws, rules and regulations that limit us to do certain things in certain ways, we might have to reconsider the whole idea of this kind of control.

As Plato stated: **"Good people do not need laws to tell them to act responsibly, while bad people will find a way around the laws."**

Much too often, a few spoil it for the rest of us. But is this a good approach for people that are essentially good?!

Well, I don't think so. Because who is to tell anyone what is right or wrong, who has the wisdom to know what's good for everyone?

I am just a child, but even though we have all these laws I feel that too many things are going wrong and I truly believe that the world is ready for real changes.

"We can't solve problems by using the same kind of thinking we used when we created them". Albert Einstein was one of history's greatest minds and even though he is more known for his achievements in physics he was a great philosopher as he eventually realized that there is so much more than meets the eye and we are able to comprehend.

> "Any fool can make things
> bigger, more complex,
> and more violent.
> It takes a touch of genius–and a
> lot of courage to move in the
> opposite direction."
>
> -
>
> Business Insider Australia

With all these amazing and very clever people with years of studies, experience and their wisdom and realisations, the world is still at a loss for getting it right. Even though we seem to know the answers we don't seem to be able to act upon them.

I feel that we are being manipulated in every facet of our lives in one way or another and I am very saddened by the inaction of people in power and our so called leaders to make things right for the benefit of everyone. We have all been created equal in the face of the divine and somehow I don't understand why we are still denying ourselves our unique potentiality.

Psychological
manipulation can be defined
as the exercise of undue
influence through mental
distortion and emotional
exploitation,
with the intention
to seize power, control,
benefits and/or privileges
at the victim's expense.

-

Psychology Today

Grounding and Hidden Meanings

Grounding yourself means stabilising your energy in your physical and mental body. It helps you secure and control your life with the right intentions.

Grounding helps you to protect yourself from being vulnerable to outside influences.

With grounding yourself you can stay present in the current moment. You might find yourself 'absent minded' or helpless if you don't ground yourself.

There are different grounding exercises you can perform.

Personally, I like to envision either roots spiralling down from my feet into mother earth or filling my soul with golden light and repeating a mantra, such as: "Through the power of divine light, divine love and divine truth I am now grounded, which I have learned from my fairy godmother, Libby Gordon.

If you do feel absent minded and/or a little lost or drained and you would like to do grounding exercises I recommend you research online, since there are plenty of different practises to choose from, and by picking one that helps you the most will help with the accuracy and intensity of it working.

Another really helpful tool to restore lack of energy

is by hugging a tree.

Yes, you read right, a tree.

Trees have been a sacred symbol in many cultures for thousands of years. Take for example the decorating of our Christmas trees, the evergreen tree was an ancient symbol of life in the midst of winter.

'Pope John Paul called the Christmas tree a symbol of Christ. This very ancient custom, he said, exalts the value of life, as in winter what is evergreen becomes a sign of undying life, and it reminds Christians of the "tree of life" of Genesis 2:9, an image of Christ, the supreme gift of God to humanity.'

Physically they provide us with oxygen and shade, and are home to animals and much more. But the effects it has on us humans mentally and emotionally, is purely spectacular. Trees, just like us, have an energy frequency or vibration as well as an aura. Their deeper, slower and somewhat more patient vibration resonates with a feeling of security, stability and safety.

When you are around trees you are colliding with the energy that they are emanating enabling you to feel grounded.

A child naturally feels drawn to trees and has an urge to climb them and spending time in a tree house. This generates excitement and wholesome happiness.

We are all drawn to trees. We enjoy sitting under them on a nice sunny day, reading a book and relaxing or even walking in the forest. A feeling of tranquillity consumes your body and makes you feel whole again.

So next time you feel down, go hug a tree.

3D to 5D

At this moment in time the world is in transition. That's why for many of us there have been a lot of radical changes.

Most people are still stuck in the 3D (third dimensional) world, meaning that they let fear and worry be the dominating force to continue on their path to their so called 'unchangeable future'. They believe to be powerless due to their entrenched ways of thinking. However, the fifth Dimensional reality is purely based on the universal laws of pure potentiality, knowing that we are the creators of our lives.

Dimensions are not places or locations, they are levels of consciousness vibrating each at a higher rate than the prior. Humanity is slowly but surely adapting to the expansion into higher dimensions.

Brief description of dimensions:
1st dimension is a line.
2nd dimension includes length and width, no understanding of up and down.
3rd dimension contains length, width and depth.
4th dimension includes movement and 'time' as we know it.
5th dimension brakes out of time, living without the linear.

When we know we can change
ourselves,
we are letting go of fear.

What is fear?
False Evidence Appearing Real

The fifth dimension is referred to the dimension of love. It is said to be the dimension of no sorrow, no anger, no fear, where no guilt exists - sounds like a dream come true?!

Through my own experiences I see the 5D world as a step beyond time, the feeling you get when something is too incredible to be real, too good to be true. The thought of something so big it's hard to imagine. Explaining the 5th dimensional world is difficult since we don't have the language yet, (or have we forgotten it?). 5D is purely based on the premise of your highest possible being. It's relatable to a feeling of utter bliss and complete knowledge of life.

To really explain it is like the feeling where you can't quite put your finger on it, but you know it's there. It's like saying something in your head. Go ahead, say any word. "..." Alright, done? Now where did you hear that word - in your head? Around your head? It was your voice, yet you physically did not speak it. You heard it, yet not with your ears. So where did it come from? And what is it?

Well that is 5D.

The dangers of Labelling

This generation and the generations that are coming through now are resonating on a much higher vibrational frequency.

Experiencing a higher state of consciousness as a child can be very confusing. Without the knowledge and understanding of it, they might face various difficulties which in turn will be misinterpreted into so called dis-eases.

Children now are more aware of systems that lack integrity and the cycle of negativity. All this is playing out on an unconscious level, that's why so many of them are lost and confused and feel the burden of all that is wrong. They feel the hypocrisy of it all but have a hard time understanding what they are actually feeling.

We see this also in the lack of interest at school. The children do not accommodate a system that is limiting and directing them into something that is completely past its use by date.

At school we are only accumulating more 'borrowed' and very limited knowledge - memorising and regurgitating lots of information thus diminishing our individual creative talents and the importance of our well-being and happiness.

Children of today find it difficult to agree with the ways schools want them to learn in the traditional way not considering their expanded way of perception. For them there is no grey zone in life, they either see white or black. Lie or truth. No in-betweens. They don't put up with it. So adults presume them as misfits, lazy or unmotivated, or even labelling them with anxiety and depression.

What we need to understand is that our children do not need help because they have 'issues', what they do need is the right guidance to make them excel in life and their highly sensitive, expanded way of perceiving the world. Using their qualities to transform the world with their unique personality into a world filled with love.

This realisation lead me to study the Indigo, Crystal, Rainbow and Star children. These children all have different qualities but they are all here to raise our collective consciousness and therefore to change the world.

If you are interested in learning more about these children, and most probably you are one of them, then I highly recommend reading "Wisdom's Children" by Lin Northrup, M.ED.

All of these kids have amazing potential but if they are not in the right environment they will shut down or be shut down usually through medication. Parents will be venturing into unfamiliar territory with these children but as scary this might be, you have to be patient, love them unconditionally and be very forgiving.

So many of us have been misdiagnosed or used as lab rats. Take ADHD for example. Children with higher sensitivity and higher vibrational frequency are transferring information faster and differently and in order to focus, they need to be in constant movement. They do not have a 'problem', they just are what they are. No labels!

In an article of the German publication 'Der Spiegel', Dr Leon Eisenberg was quoted saying: "ADHD is a prime example of a fictitious disease". He was a child psychiatry researcher and one of the first to advocate major research studies on children's developmental problems, like ADHA and autism.

Labels are harmful and limiting and only serve to judge someone or something. Once labelled one carries the heavy burden of being diminished to only that description.

Deeming our children to having a 'problem' and having a 'disorder' or 'disease', we burden them with negative attachments.

What ever happened to simply being sad? We are not leaving any room to just be sad anymore. We are humans after all and we need to understand that sadness is only an emotion just like happiness. But at the end of the day it's the one you decide on.

Connection

With all that I have gone through and the doubts and uncertainties I have experienced, I had one constant in my life, and that was and is my mum. I am very fortunate to have a really powerful connection with her and that she guides me through real leadership. She is not all talk but actually acts upon her words, which lead me to being the person that I am today.

I truly believe that we all need someone in our lives that we can look up to, someone that inspires you and gives you direction.

Someone you can aspire to be.

You develop respect for that someone that leads you through actions and not only talk. Watching them deal with life in a positive way, facing all challenges head-on and never giving up will drive you to strive for excellence and to keep trying to be the best version of yourself.

Having this figure in your life keeps you on track when you feel low or unmotivated. You don't want to let them down, so you push yourself that little bit harder. When you feel unconditional love then you will understand when this person gives you boundaries and you will more easily comply with what he or she is asking of you.

Unfortunately I have witnessed too often that there is a total lack of connection between parents and children and therefore peers amongst each other.

With the extensive use of social media we seem to be more connected, but it's only always through a screen. It's not REAL. It's basically an artificial connection.

We are losing the natural way of communicating and addressing each other respectfully and with some thought behind our words. You can hide behind a quickly sent text or message/email. It's much more challenging to communicate face to face.

We need to be able to view a person holistically, being able to interpret their body language, facial expressions, etc. in order to 'read' the person properly, otherwise we might miss the cue that they are actually uncomfortable or upset with what we say to them.

It's all about how you make someone feel and you should always only make someone feel good about themselves, because it actually comes back to you.

When both parents are at work all day and the children don't really have much time with them, both parties miss out on precious and important time together. I really believe that people put too much pressure on themselves to 'give' their children everything – but this everything is sadly in the materialistic arena. What we children really need is TIME, and plenty of that. Time seems precious these days, but the times you miss out on being there for your child when it needs you most, can never be made up.

In order to gain respect you need to show respect. Everything is mutual. Whatever you give out, you will receive.

Making time for children shows them that you care, that you love them, that they mean the world to you. I wonder sometimes why parents work so hard to make that much more money to then literally 'park' their child at the closest facility for that extra earned amount of money, then feeling guilty for not being around and then buying their love back with more money.

Your child will only remember the presence you bestowed on them not the presents you bought them.

And when the children are older and they come home to an empty house, they feel empty inside.

Deep connection needs to be recognised as a highly important aspect in your child's well-being.

Ykids Hub

So many of my friends have very hard times coping with life. And sadly, some just couldn't deal with life at all.

They don't know what they are capable of, what treasures they carry inside and how beautiful they are. They don't trust their instincts and they don't feel worthy or special. They are surrounded by negativity and restrictions, limitations and hypocrisy.

They feel the pressures of an ever faster changing and demanding world that does not make sense any more. They are lost and confused, feeling sad and frustrated. Most of them are on real heavy drugs to calm them down, sedate them, motivate them or ease their pain. Every minor incident or feeling gets addressed with a major chemical bomb which in turn plays on their mind.

By administering drugs to young people we are not addressing the underlying issues that cause their mental and other pain. Everything is inter-connected and cannot be fixed by some wonder pill.

All those hospital visits due to my seizures, made me realise, that too many of us are misunderstood, misjudged and misdiagnosed.

Every doctor wanted me to believe that I had anxiety and depression and that I had some sort of issue, because they did not find anything wrong with me from a medical perspective. And that there is a lot between heaven and earth we do not take into consideration or don't even talk about in the open.

My experiences allow me to view and feel the world and its people as one of its pure source. Where the past, present and future selves are being weighed down with unneeded confining beliefs.

The real issue with young people today is their heightened sensitivity and their higher emotional and spiritual intelligence. They feel the pressure of all the grief and pain and all that's wrong in the world and has been for too long.

All this time we have been blinded to our brilliance, ignorant of our true selves and unaware of our true power and magnificence.

I see a brighter future by investing into the children who hold the key as their innocence and deeper connectedness is what this world needs. And we will do this through the creation of Y-kids hubs - an awe inspiring place that allows for creativity, exploration and play,

a space filled with colour, laughter and fun,
a place where children can go to feel very special,
wanted and needed and build on their own talents.

Children need a strong root system to develop their
beautiful minds and bodies and to realise their true
potential and the Y-kids hub will facilitate and support
every effort into developing the right tools to create

...**a world** with no limiting beliefs where we are not
defined by labels but by our uniqueness.

...**a world** that is connected, loving, accepting,
respectful and supportive of each other with room
for everyone to be who he or she needs to be for the
highest possible good for **all** concerned.

I believe that children - actually all of us - carry all
the wisdom and knowledge inside themselves. But
in order to achieve their full potential you need to
add love and attention and create a positive, beautiful
environment where there is room for unleashing the
true YOU.

I can't stress it enough; It is so important to make
time for children, so they know that you care, to live
what you preach and love them unconditionally. I urge
everyone to re-evaluate what you have come to belief
to be true and real and whether what others tell you is
the way to go. Trust your instincts and that inner voice

that will guide you in the right direction. Know it and own it.

Just like I learned from the one story, showing gratitude and taking full responsibility for anything you say, do or feel, you will no longer allow yourself to blame someone or something for your misfortune, your sadness, anything that is detrimental to your well-being and happiness.

We are creators, we are not sheep and we don't need to wait for anyone to show or tell us where we need to go and what we need to do. History will keep repeating itself until we step out and up. It's time to take charge of ourselves and create a happy, well-balanced, thriving individual in a nurturing, beautiful environment.

Thank you

Lightning Source UK Ltd.
Milton Keynes UK
UKHW03f0627180418
321252UK00001B/258/P